A CLEAN PLANET:

THE SOLAR POWER STORY

Robyn C. Friend
and
Judith Love Cohen

ILLUSTRATIONS:
David A. Katz

Compliments of

DOW CORNING
Dow Corning
Foundation

Cascade
Pass, Inc.
www.CascadePass.com

Editing:
Lee Rathbone

Copyright © 2009 by Cascade Pass, Inc.
Published by Cascade Pass, Inc.
4223 Glencoe Avenue, Suite C-105
Marina del Rey, CA 90292-8801
Phone: (310) 305-0210
Web Site: http://www.CascadePass.com
Printed in China by South China Printing Co. Ltd.

First Edition 2009

A Clean Planet: The Solar Power Story was written by Robyn C. Friend and Judith Love Cohen, and edited by Lee Rathbone. Designed and illustrated by David Katz.

This book is one of a series that emphasizes the environment and the value of preserving it by depicting what real people are doing to meet the challenges.

Other books in the series include:
A Clean City: The Green Construction Story
A Clean Sky: The Global Warming Story
A Clean Sea: The Rachel Carson Story

Library of Congress Cataloging-in-Publication Data

Friend, Robyn C., 1955-
    A Clean Planet : the Solar Power Story / Robyn C. Friend and Judith Love Cohen ; edited by Lee Rathbone.
    p. cm.
    ISBN 1-880599-86-4 (pbk.) – ISBN 1-880599-87-2 (hard cover)
    1. Solar energy–Juvenile literature. I. Cohen, Judith Love, 1933-. II. Rathbone, Lee. III. Title.

TJ810.3.F75 2009
621.47–dc22
        2009004908

Introduction

The sun is the most important source of energy for all life on Earth. We use the sun's energy every day in many different ways. Its huge supply of energy keeps us warm, grows our food, and provides light during our day. This book tells the story of solar power (energy from the sun), what it is, what it can do, and how we can use it to help us have a cleaner planet.

This is the fourth book in Cascade Pass's environmental series dedicated to the resources of our planet Earth – the oceans, the skies, the rainforests, the deserts… all those special environments that are shared by varieties of animals and plants – and to those whose efforts protect them. *A Clean Planet: The Solar Power Story* explains the power of the sun, its importance to sustaining life, and how we are starting to utilize its energy to replace the sources of energy used today which are damaging our environment.

When you woke up this morning was the sun shining? Or was it cloudy? No matter what, light may have peeked through your window, or perhaps through a window in another room, and you knew it was daylight outside. How come? Because the sun gives us light whether it is bright and sunny or gloomy and cloudy.

The sun is a powerful source of energy. It is easy to take the benefits that the sun provides for granted because it is always there. The sun not only gives us light, it also warms us, supplies the energy that makes plants grow, makes rain, creates the oxygen that we breathe, and powers the winds. The sun is what makes weather and climate changes. Without the sun there could be no life at all on the earth.

You might be wondering how the sun can do all these things. As an example, let's take a look at rain, and how the sun affects weather.

When the sun shines on water, it heats up and becomes water vapor. This water vapor turns into clouds, and when they cool down again, we have rain!! So you can see that without the sun, we wouldn't have rain.

But what about wind?

When the air is hot in one place and cold in another, the air in the hotter place expands and pushes the colder air. This makes wind and other forms of weather patterns. Perhaps, you may have heard a **meteorologist** (meet-ee-ur-ahl-o-jist) talk about weather patterns on the news.

SUNSHINE

CLOUDS

The sun
affects
the weather.

RAIN

WIND

The sun affects animals and plants even more directly. By using the power of the sun, plants turn decomposed plant material (like leaves or fruit) and rainwater into the things we all need to live, like food to eat and the part of the air that we breathe, oxygen.

If you want a plant to grow, you need to give it plenty of sun and water. How does this work? Sunlight provides energy for plants to grow. Through a wonderful process called *photosynthesis* (fot-o-sin-the-sis), plants are able to take energy from the sun and create sugars. Through photosynthesis plants are able to store energy from the sunlight in chemical bonds that can be used later. As a result, plants give off oxygen into the air which we breathe in, and when we breathe it out it turns to carbon dioxide.

It's a continuous cycle; plants combine the carbon dioxide produced by animals and humans with the energy from sunlight to make oxygen over and over again.

Plants
use
the power of
the sun.

People have been using the sun's energy for many years, both *directly* and *indirectly*.

We use the sun *indirectly* when we use the plants that were grown by photosynthesis. When people or animals eat, they are using solar energy *indirectly*.

When wood that is cut from a tree is burned, we are using solar energy *indirectly*. When materials known as fossil fuels (oil, natural gas or coal) are burned, solar energy is used *indirectly*, by making use of energy from the sun that was captured centuries ago.

Burning wood
uses solar energy
indirectly.

Using the sun's energy **directly** means using it as it soon as it shines.

Thousands of years ago, the Greeks and the Chinese learned that the sun provided more heat and light when facing south. They used this knowledge and built their buildings facing south, so that the buildings would receive more light and warmth from the sun.

When you hang your freshly washed clothes or wet swim suit in the sun you are using the sun's energy **directly** to dry them. The process that the sun uses to dry the clothes and your swim suit is called **evaporation** (ee-vap-uh-ray-shun).

Using the Sun's Energy Directly!

There are two newer, more *efficient* ways that we can use the energy from the sun for our energy needs.

One *indirect* way is called *solar thermal*. We use the sun's energy hitting earth by capturing it as heat, like when we use solar panels to heat water.

Another *indirect* way to get the sun's energy is by use of *Photovoltaic* (fot-o-vol-tay-ik) *Cells* (or PV cells for short); with this process sunlight energy is captured and converted to electrical energy. More than 150 years ago, the first photovoltaic solar cell was constructed. Photovoltaic cells convert sunlight into electrical current. PV cells can be found on many small electronic devices like calculators and watches.

In 1958, the United States launched a satellite, Vanguard I, which was powered by a chemical battery. This battery is like the ones found in MP3 players, but it also had solar cells as a backup power source. The solar cells worked so well that the satellite continued to transmit data for a year after its chemical battery was used up. Since then, solar cells have been used in many other satellites, and have become the main source of power for most space vehicles.

Photovoltaic
Solar Cells
on a Satellite

The early solar cells were very expensive and *inefficient*. They did not generate very much electricity. Since then, scientists and engineers have learned to build cells that are more *efficient*, creating a lot of electricity with a small amount of sunlight.

Today, solar cells have become less expensive and reliable enough to use in our homes, while conventional power sources, such as oil, have become more expensive. Because solar power generates no additional pollution after installation, governments sometimes offer to help pay for solar cells, to encourage people to put them on their houses.

A good example of how solar energy is being used is at a Midland, Michigan baseball field. Solar panels are providing energy to power the scoreboard.

Michigan Baseball Field
Using Solar Energy
to Power the Scoreboard

Because there is no need to lay long power lines, solar cells can be used in very remote places where electricity is too expensive. Solar cells can generate electricity for homes and even entire villages, providing lights to help people read, pumps to help move water for crops, and refrigeration for food and medicine. The electrical energy from solar cells can be stored in batteries to light a roadside billboard or power a cell phone when no telephone wires are available.

The more that people use solar cells to generate electricity in their houses and businesses, the less expensive solar cells will become. Continuing advances in equipment, materials, and manufacturing processes make it possible to produce solar cells for less money, making them more affordable.

Solar cells are made mostly of an *element* called *silicon* (sil-i-ken). This is the same element that is found in beach sand and is the main ingredient in glass.

Perhaps you are wondering: how can the silicon in beach sand turn sunlight into electricity? Silicon is a *semi-conductor*, a solid material that *conducts electricity* under some conditions, and not under others.

Polysilicon is used
in solar cells.

How do we turn grains of sand into solar cells to generate electricity?

Let's look at how high-purity *polysilicon* is made into solar cells at a company called Hemlock Semiconductor. First, everything in the beach sand that is not silicon must be removed. This is because even the smallest amount of impurities can get in the way of electrons moving in the solar cell.

The process begins when the silicon in either sand or quartz is heated in a furnace until it becomes liquid. The oxygen in the sand is chemically removed. When the liquid cools, the silicon looks like lumps of shiny gray rocks. Those rocks are then ground into small chunks, and a chemical is added to make it a liquid that is *purified* or *distilled*. This removes any left-over impurities from the sand.

This process is repeated until all that remains is pure silicon.

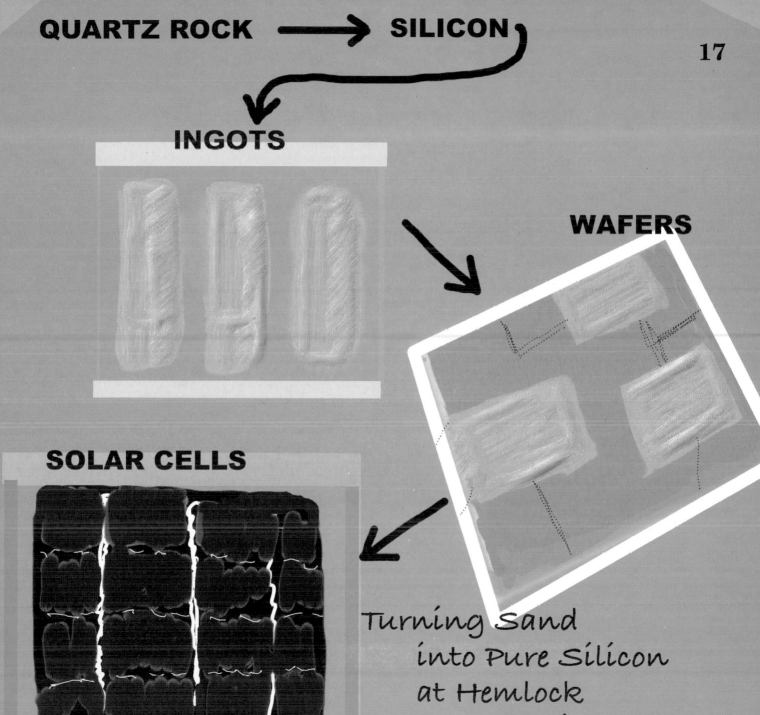

QUARTZ ROCK → SILICON

INGOTS

WAFERS

SOLAR CELLS

Turning Sand
into Pure Silicon
at Hemlock
Semiconductor

The next step is to convert the pure silicon-containing gas to a solid: ***polycrystalline silicon***. It's similar to when you make a candle by dipping a string in melted wax over and over. Eventually, the string gets coated with thicker and thicker layers of wax until you have a candle. The silicon ***atoms*** in the gas keep sticking onto each other forming a rod of pure polycrystalline silicon that grows bigger and bigger. This highly pure silicon will be the active part of the solar device, allowing sunlight to be absorbed and converted to flowing electrons.

The silicon rods are then melted down and cooled to form a ***crystal***. A crystal is a solid, like ice or metal with a very precise arrangement of the individual atoms. For example, a snowflake is a crystal made of frozen water. The pure silicon crystals then are sliced into very thin wafers so that the most sunlight can be absorbed over a large area.

To make the silicon wafer into a solar cell, wires and circuitry are attached to them so that the electrons excited by light from the sun can be collected, stored, or used as electric power. All those silicon electrons get sent down the wires to run your washing machine or your lights, and return back again, by the other wire in the loop.

Pure silicon allows sunlight
to be absorbed and
converted to flowing electrons.

Solar energy comes from the sun, but what about ***electricity***? You know what happens when you flip the light switch in your room: electric current flows to the light bulb, and the light turns on. *Electricity* is the flow of electrons from a power source to an object that reacts to the flow of electrons by moving or lighting up. Electricity is a train of electrons pushing other electrons down a wire.

What makes the electrons flow?

Think of popping popcorn in your microwave oven: the microwave heats the corn kernels and pretty soon they start hopping around inside the bag. When sunlight reaches the solar cell it excites the electrons in the silicon. The sunlight makes them zip around really fast like the microwave popcorn kernels, and turns the silicon into a rich source of usable electrons. Wires attached to the solar cell act like a drainpipe, and move those excited electrons along the wire to where they can be used ***directly*** as electricity, or ***indirectly***, by storing it in a battery to use later.

Electrons
Hopping
onto Wire

One difference between the microwave popcorn and the electrons is that, unlike the popcorn in the bag, the electrons will flow only when there is a full, closed loop.

The process works like a merry-go-round. The sun excites the electrons in the solar cell. Then the excited electrons push down the wire to the light bulb, heat the *filament* in the light bulb, causing the filament to glow, which is the light that we see. Then the electrons go down another wire back to the other side of the solar cell. In other words, the electrons ride the merry-go-round back to where they started (it goes around and around). Electricity will not flow without a complete loop.

Look at an electric plug – there are at least two wires, one wire to bring the electricity from the source to the appliance that will use it, and the second wire to bring the electricity back to the other side of the source.

Electrons light the bulb!

How does this help our Planet Earth stay cleaner?

What are the many benefits of electricity, and the many everyday things for which you use it? We use it to light our world at night; to preserve our food; to wash and dry dishes, clothes, and people; to power medical equipment that helps sick people; to power the machines and tools we use to build our homes and offices; to manufacture everything we use including our toys, cell phone chargers and television sets.

But we can choose the method we use to generate electricity. One of the easiest and natural ways we do this is through solar energy.

Solar energy is "clean," meaning that once the solar cells have been made and installed, using them doesn't add carbon dioxide or other pollutants to the air. Solar energy is quiet and requires very little maintenance. And a crystalline silicon solar cell can produce energy this way for more than 30 years! When we use energy generated from solar power, less power needs to be generated from burning fuels like wood, oil, or coal that dirty the air.

In places where homes and offices are not connected to a **_power grid_**, the electricity can be either used directly, or stored in a battery to be used later. In places where homes and offices are connected to a power grid, any unused electricity gets sent out to the power grid for someone else to use.

Solar cell farms reduce
the amount of energy
we need to get from
the electric company.

You Can Help!

As more people begin to use solar energy, we will have less pollution and will conserve precious oil, coal, and natural gas. You can help discover solar energy solutions by becoming a scientist or engineer. You can make better, more efficient, solar cells for the future: ones that can generate more electricity from the same amount of sunlight. You can help make them less expensive, so more people can afford to buy them, and you can help make it possible for solar energy to be used in parts of the world that don't have access to other forms of power generation.

Here are some careers in solar energy that you can think about for your future!

Architect: An architect designs buildings and structures. As an architect, you could design beautiful and practical new ways to use solar cells and solar-powered energy systems in the structure and design of buildings, making them attractive and reliable.

Building Contractor: As a building contractor, you would work with an architect to construct buildings with solar-powered energy systems.

Chemist: Chemistry is the study of the composition, structure, and properties of substances, and the transformations they undergo. As a chemist, you might study how to make solar cells, trying to devise

People Working on Solar Energy

new methods that will make the cells last longer, be more efficient, and cost less.

Electrician: As an electrician, you could work with a building contractor installing solar cells and solar-powered energy systems.

Engineer: Engineering uses mathematics and the sciences to design, analyze, and construct projects. As an engineer, you might invent new ways to make solar cells that use less power, cost less to manufacture, and create less waste materials. There are many different kinds of engineers that combine different sciences with engineering to create new solutions

As a **Chemical Engineer** you could combine the knowledge of chemistry and engineering to develop new manufacturing processes.

As a **Civil Engineer** you could find new ways to incorporate solar cells into all kinds of public structures – office buildings, warehouses, and museums.

As an **Electrical Engineer** you could develop ways to make the appliances that use solar energy more efficient.

As a **Mechanical Engineer** you could design ways to mount solar cells on houses that are safer, last longer, and are less expensive.

Geologist: Geology is the study of the Earth. It includes the study of the composition, structure, physical properties, dynamics, and history of Earth materials, and how they are formed, moved, and changed. As a geologist, you could discover new sources for the materials needed to make solar cells.

Materials Scientist: Materials Science is the study of what things are made of and what their characteristics are. It involves how things are created chemically, how they behave when you try to bend them or melt them, and how they can be used in a device or a process. As a materials scientist, you could combine the knowledge of applied physics and chemistry, as well as chemical, mechanical, civil and electrical engineering. to improve the manufacturing and use of solar cells.

Metallurgist: Metallurgy is the study of the physical and chemical behavior of metallic elements and *compounds* (compounds of metals are called alloys), and the ways metals can be used in technology. As a metallurgist, you might find ways to make silicon-based solar cells more efficient or last longer.

Physicist: Physics is the study of matter and its motion. It includes the study of very basic concepts such as force, energy, mass, and charge, and how all forms of matter behave. As a physicist, you might improve our basic understanding of the movement of electrons in a material, leading to new ways to build solar cells that are more efficient, last longer, and cost less.

Now you know how solar cells are made and what different scientists do to make the solar cells work better. If you work hard in school and study the sciences, you can help make solar cells work better, too!

FUN FACTS

Fun Fact 1: Did you know that the most abundant mineral on the surface of the earth is sand?
That means that there is plenty of silicon available to make solar cells!

Fun Fact 2: Did you know that solar power has a low negative impact on the environment?

The environmental impact of solar power is low. Solar is clean power. There are no emissions, and no unstable fuel costs. Solar power is reliable, with no outages. It is a free source of energy, unlike oil, coal, or natural gas. Saving money, conserving energy, and producing clean power are the best benefits of solar energy. Clean power is collected throughout the daytime, with excess power stored in batteries for use later.

Fun Fact 3: Did you know photovoltaic cells (PV Cells) have two layers of semi-conductors?

One is positively charged and the other is negatively charged. When these two semi-conductors absorb light their electrons get excited. The negatively and positively charged particles flowing from these semi-conductors then create tension or volts, which create more light and more electricity. As long as you have enough PV cells working, a PV solar panel can turn on your lights, equipment, and basically anything that uses electricity.

Fun Fact 4: Did you know solar power is beneficial in many ways?

There are no moving parts to replace or break. Solar panels are strong, and can last through extreme weather conditions, including heat and cold, humidity, and even hail storms. Solar powered systems work well in many areas: on homes and offices, for street lights, and for outdoor signs. There are even small solar panels that are portable and easy to carry. You can use these when going out on adventures like camping.

Fun Fact 5: Did you know that most of the electronics in the world – computers, cars, video games, and everything – use polycrystalline silicon, similar to that in solar cells?

Fun Fact 6: In approximately two years, a solar cell can generate more energy than was used to manufacture it!

Fun Fact 7: There is enough solar energy hitting the surface of the earth in one hour to supply the electricity needs of the world's population for one year.

Fun Fact 8: Did you know that you can use the power of the sun directly to cook food?

Go to this website to find out how you can make your own pizza box cooker, but be sure to get help from an adult! http://www.reachoutmichigan.org/funexperiments/agesubject/lessons/other/solar.html

For more about solar cookers, visit: http://solarcookers.org/basics/how.html

Fun Fact 9: Solar power can be used for lots of fun things!

Experimental planes that fly using solar power have made some exciting flights! You can read more about them at http://news.bbc.co.uk/2/hi/science/nature/6916309.stm

To read how one man built a solar power system for his camper, go to http://www.otherpower.com/popup.html

To find out more about the second American satellite, Vanguard I, visit this site: http://www.spacedaily.com/news/satellite-tech-03c.html

Glossary

Atom: The smallest particle of an element that can exist either alone or in combination.

Compound: A chemical or substance that is composed of more than one type of atom; for example, water, which is composed of groupings (called molecules) that each consist of one hydrogen atom and two oxygen atoms.

Conducts Electricity: Transmission of electrical energy.

Crystal: A body formed by the solidification of a chemical element or compound with regularly repeating patterns of atoms.

Directly: Using the sun's energy directly means without storing it up to use later. Some examples are drying clothes on a laundry line in the sun, designing a building so that the sun shines in to warm up the inside, and using the heat of the sun to cook food.

Distilled: A distilled liquid has been purified by heating and condensing it, until all that is left is a collection of the purified liquid, with whatever is undesirable left behind in the heating pan as a solid.

Efficient: Efficient means productive with relatively less waste. Solar cells currently in production convert only about 10% of the energy in the sunlight that hits them into electricity; the remaining 90% of that energy is wasted. We say that those solar cells are "10% efficient." As we learn to build solar cells that convert more of the energy in the sunlight that hits them into electricity, it will mean those new solar cells are "more efficient." Solar cells in laboratories can sometimes convert as much as 25% of the light that hits them into electricity.

Electricity: The flow of electrons from a power source to an object (and back).

Element: A substance that consists of atoms of only one kind (as opposed to a compound, which is composed of different kinds of atoms) for example, oxygen, which is composed of only oxygen atoms.

Evaporation: A process where heat turns water from a liquid into a gas.

Filament: A filament is a single thread or a thread-like object, like a thin wire. A metal filament can conduct electrons.

Indirectly: Using the sun's energy indirectly means that the energy is stored up to be used later, like using solar cells to collect the energy and then sending the energy to be stored in a battery so it can be used at another time.

Meteorologist: Scientist who studies the Earth's atmosphere and weather.

Photosynthesis: A process that plants use to take in carbon dioxide from the air and nitrogen from the ground, and (using energy from the sun), use that carbon and nitrogen to create more plant parts: leaves, stems, fruits and vegetables. As a by-product, the plants give off the oxygen.

Photovoltaic cells: The prefix photo- means "light". The root voltaic means "energy potential." Photovoltaic cells are thin crystals of silicon (or other materials) that take light from the sun, and convert it directly into electrical energy.

Polycrystalline silicon: The purest man made material consisting of multiple small silicon crystals.

Power grid: The totality of the poles, wires, transformers, and control equipment that distributes electric power in an area.

Purified: Freed from anything that debases, pollutes, adulterates, or contaminates a substance.

Semi-conductor: A solid material that has electrical conductivity between those of a conductor and an insulator; the extent of electrical conductivity can vary over that wide range, either permanently or dynamically.

Silicon: An element that exhibits properties intermediate between a metal and a non-metal. It is the second most abundant element on the earth's surface, after oxygen.

Solar thermal: A way of using the sun's energy indirectly, by capturing the sun's rays in the form of heat as it shines on the surface of the Earth, and using that heat to perform other useful work, such as heating water.

A CLEAN PLANET: THE SOLAR POWER STORY

LESSON PLAN 1

PURPOSE: To begin to understand how the separate elements are combined into compounds.

MATERIALS: List of elements, list of common compounds, package of various colored gumdrops, box of toothpicks.

PROCEDURES: Have the children separate the gumdrops by color. Have them pick a few compounds from the list provided. (e. g. Sodium Chloride (table salt); Di-Hydrogen oxide (water); Carbon Monoxide).

Have the children select a color for each element in the compounds chosen (Hydrogen, Carbon, Oxygen, Sodium, Chlorine).

Have the children use toothpicks to connect the gumdrops representing individual elements. One Oxygen element and two Hydrogen elements can be connected with two toothpicks; one Carbon element and one Oxygen element can be connected with one toothpick; One Sodium element and one Chlorine element are connected with one toothpick. Each model represents a molecule of the compound.

CONCLUSIONS: What does the chemical formula H_2O represent?
What do the numbers in formulas mean?
What do the letters mean?
(H_2O represents water, the H is the symbol for Hydrogen, the O is the symbol for Oxygen and the "2" means that there are two atoms of Hydrogen and one atom of Oxygen in a water molecule.)

RESOURCES: Periodic Table or Library books such as *The Usborne Book of Science*.

LESSON PLAN 2

PURPOSE: To understand where solar cell farms are placed and what they look like.

MATERIALS: Scissors, glue, shoe boxes, art supplies (paper, crayons, paints, colored pencils and glitter).

PROCEDURE: Have children take the shoe box and create an area that will contain a solar farm: open fields, deserts, large open spaces etc. but surrounded by mountains, forests, or other remote areas. They should create large scale solar arrays. Solar arrays should be shown in their proper environments. And remember there is lots of sun!

CONCLUSIONS: Why are solar array farms located in remote areas?
Why do they all face the same way?

RESOURCES: Pictures of various solar farms from the internet.

LESSON PLAN 3

PURPOSE: To learn about growing plants and the importance of plants.

MATERIALS: Styrofoam cups, potting material, seeds, little shovel, growing instructions.

PROCEDURE: Discuss how different plants like different kinds of environments, some plants like lots of water, others like less, some plants like lots of sun, others prefer shade, some plants like it warm, others like less warmth. Always read the seed directions for what your plant needs. Have each child fill their styrofoam cup half full with potting compound or soil, use ruler or transplanter to dig a hole of right depth, put seed in cup and cover. Discuss how and when to transplant plant and how to care for it. Show how plants protect themselves: (roses grow thorns, garlic stinks). What other examples can you think of?

CONCLUSIONS: Does your plant need to be in the shade?
How often should you water it?
When will you know it is time to transplant it?

ABOUT THE CONTRIBUTORS:

DON BUCHALSKI, contributor is a Senior Marketing Specialist for the Photovoltaic Industry within Dow Corning's Solar Market Business Unit. Based at Dow Corning's Solar Solutions Application Center in Freeland, Michigan, he is responsible for defining and leading the implementation of Dow Corning's commercial and marketing strategies for the PV Module Assembly & Integration Segments. Don joined Dow Corning in 1986 as a process design engineer. Since then, he has held a number of positions in process engineering, manufacturing, supply chain logistics and marketing. He took on the strategic marketing responsibility for photovoltaics in 2007. Don received his Bachelor of Science degree in chemical engineering from Michigan Technological University in 1986 and his M.B.A. from the University of Michigan – Flint in 1991.

GREG BAUSCH, contributor is the Solar Application and Technical Service Manager at Hemlock Semiconductor Group. Greg is a chemist and worked in several different Science and Technology (S&T) roles at Dow Corning Corporation for 21 years prior to coming to Hemlock Semiconductor, including four years leading S&T for the solar program. Greg holds five patents, and has numerous external publications focused on Dow Corning materials development, and several industries including life sciences and coatings. Greg hopes this book will inspire children everywhere to get excited and engaged in science and technology.

ETHAN GOOD, contributor is widely recognized as an expert in silicon crystal growth and solar device fabrication. He is a materials scientist who has worked in various areas from military systems to elastomeric compounding before joining the solar industry over 10 years ago. He earned a B.S. in Metallurgical and Materials Engineering and a Ph.D. in Materials Science at the Colorado School of Mines. He enjoys the awesome power of the sun while kayaking and mountain biking with his wife Jessica.

DAVE PASEK, contributor is the Science & Technology Director for Hemlock Semiconductor Group. He has held a variety of engineering and leadership positions within Hemlock Semiconductor and Dow Corning. He holds a B.S. in Chemical Engineering from the University of Minnesota. He resides in Michigan with his wife and three children, and enjoys reading books with them every day.

ABOUT THE AUTHORS:

ROBYN C. FRIEND, author is a singer, dancer, choreographer, and writer. She earned a Ph.D. in Iranian Linguistics at UCLA, and promptly launched a twenty-year career building spacecraft. She has written for both scholarly and popular publications on a wide variety of subjects, including folkloric dance, world music, linguistics, travel, and the exploration of Mars by balloon.

JUDITH LOVE COHEN, author is a Registered Professional Electrical Engineer with bachelor's and master's degrees in engineering from the University of Southern California and University of California, Los Angeles. She has written plays, screenplays, and newspaper articles in addition to her series of children's books that began with *You Can Be a Woman Engineer*.

ABOUT THE ILLUSTRATOR:

DAVID ARTHUR KATZ, illustrator received his training in art education and holds a master's degree from the University of South Florida. He is a credentialed teacher in the Los Angeles Unified School District. His involvement in the arts has encompassed animation, illustration, and playwriting, poetry, and songwriting. His drawings and animations are presently being collected in museums.

Graphic materials created by **KANA TATEKAWA**, Momo Communications, Inc.

Editorial Support provided by **LESLIE OROZCO**, Hemlock Semiconductor and **JULIE RUBIS**, JR Communiqué.

Helping to make America a 21st Century Solar Power – today.

Solar panels, like those that power the scoreboard at Dow Diamond in Midland, Michigan, rely on silicon technology to harness the power of the sun. Enabled by Dow Corning and its joint ventures, the Hemlock Semiconductor Group, this technology generates clean, renewable energy that provides warmth and light for people around the world.

We help you invent the future.™

DOW CORNING

energy saving

recycling expertise

education partnership

waste reduction

resource conservation

possibility expansion

material transformation

problem solving

opportunity creation

eco innovation

community support

local involvement

innovative thinking

knowledge sharing

sustainable solutions

environmental stewardship

Responsible Care®

How can Hemlock Semiconductor improve your community?

Transformation can be both beautiful and beneficial. At Hemlock Semiconductor Group, we're helping to transform our communities through progress that enhances math and science education, promotes health and wellness, and improves the quality of life. We're proud to be part of your community!